Journey to the future: How artificial intelligence and robotics will change our lives in 2060

Introduction
Paragraph 1:

In recent years, the term "artificial intelligence" has become popular in various fields. We hear about it in the news, see it on smartphones, and use it in apps and websites. With this great spread, people began to wonder about its nature, how it works, and can it surpass human intelligence? These questions make it important to distinguish between two types of intelligence: natural intelligence, which is possessed by humans, and artificial intelligence, which is created by machines. This distinction not only helps understand technology, but also illustrates the capabilities of humans and the limits of machines. We will begin by defining each type of intelligence, then explain the similarities and differences between them.

Paragraph 2:
Natural intelligence is what distinguishes humans from other living creatures. It is the ability of the human mind to think, analyse, solve problems, and make decisions. A person uses his natural intelligence in his daily life, whether in study, work, or dealing with others. Natural intelligence develops from childhood, and increases with experience and learning. Humans can feel, empathize, create, and imagine new things. This type of intelligence is linked to feelings and emotions, and cannot be easily imitated. Natural intelligence also allows humans to understand context and act wisely in different situations.

Paragraph 3:
Artificial intelligence is a type of intelligence that is programmed into computers and robots. AI is designed to mimic some human abilities, such as image recognition, speech understanding, gaming, or translation. Artificial intelligence does not have a mind or consciousness, but rather relies on instructions set by programmers. There are multiple types of artificial intelligence, including simple ones that perform specific tasks, and advanced ones that can learn from data. But it remains limited, because it does not think as a human thinks, but rather follows pre-programmed logical steps.

Paragraph 4:
One of the fundamental differences between natural and artificial intelligence is emotion. A person feels love, fear, sadness, and joy, and is affected by what happens around him. These feelings affect his decisions and way of thinking. As for artificial intelligence, it does not have any feelings, and it cannot understand feelings the way humans

understand them. He deals with commands and data only, and is not affected psychologically or emotionally. This makes it useful in some situations that require neutrality and speed, but it is not suitable in situations that require empathy or human understanding.

Paragraph 5:
Natural intelligence is characterized by creativity and innovation. Man is capable of writing stories, drawing pictures, composing music, and inventing things. These abilities come from his imagination and vast imagination. While AI can sometimes produce similar content, it is based on past data, and has no real imagination. Everything he does is based on what he learns from the information he is provided with. Therefore, he cannot be considered creative in the same way as humans, because he cannot create something new out of nothing.

Paragraph 6:
Artificial intelligence is characterized by its great speed in processing data and implementing operations. It can analyze millions of data in seconds, which would take a human being hours or days. Therefore, artificial intelligence is used in medicine, economics, and engineering, where it can help in making accurate and quick decisions. However, his decisions remain based on statistics and not on a true understanding of the situation. Natural intelligence, although sometimes slow, takes into account human, cultural and social factors that are difficult for artificial intelligence to understand or appreciate.

Paragraph 7:
Natural intelligence is constantly developing in humans. The more experiences a person has, the more lessons he learns, the wiser and more understanding he becomes. As for artificial intelligence, it does not develop on its own, but rather requires updates and modifications from programmers. There is an advanced type called "machine learning," which allows artificial intelligence to learn from data, but this learning is not similar to human learning. Because it remains restricted to a certain scope, and cannot depart from it. While humans can connect different fields and think in unexpected ways.

Paragraph 8:
Despite all the differences between the two types, artificial intelligence is not an enemy of human intelligence. Rather, it is a powerful tool that can

help a person and make his life easier. When used correctly, it can save time and effort, and make life more convenient and easier. But it is important for a person to learn how to balance the use of technology with maintaining his natural skills. Excessive reliance on artificial intelligence may lead to weak natural thinking, and this is what you should pay attention to.

Paragraph 9:
There are fears that artificial intelligence may threaten people's jobs, or one day control their lives. But the reality is that this depends on the way we use this technology. Humans are the ones who control artificial intelligence and set rules and limits for it. Therefore, it is necessary to use it wisely, and to preserve natural intelligence through reading, thinking, and experimenting, and not completely rely on machines. The future should not be a struggle between man and machine, but rather cooperation between the two.

Paragraph 10:
In conclusion, it can be said that natural intelligence and artificial intelligence complement each other, and one cannot replace the other. Natural intelligence is the origin, and artificial intelligence is the result of this human intelligence. Each of them has an important role in life. By understanding the differences between them, we can use AI in a beneficial way, without losing what makes us human: feeling, creativity, and wisdom. We must develop technology, but without forgetting to develop ourselves as well.

Chapter One: Artificial Intelligence in Commerce 2060
(Smart stores and marketing analytics)

Paragraph 1:
Imagine entering a store in the year 2060, and seeing no sellers, not even a cashier! Rather, the door opens for you automatically, and a smart screen greets you, calling your name, and suggesting that you buy shoes you liked a month ago. This is not science fiction, but a technological reality that is coming with a bang. Artificial intelligence has changed everything in the world of commerce, and has made the store a place that understands you more than you understand yourself! Shopping is no longer just a purchase, but an enjoyable journey led by

intelligence that understands you, anticipates you, and serves you as you like.

Paragraph 2:

In the year 2060, stores are no longer as we know them today. The walls light up depending on your mood, and products move towards you if you feel hesitant to buy them. Soft-voiced robots roam among customers, whispering exclusive offers to you, and analyzing your facial expression to understand if you're excited or not. Everything is connected, from your first glance at a product, to the moment it leaves the store. It is an intelligent, interactive world, where there is no room for chance.

Paragraph 3:

How does the store know all this about you? Simply put: through massive data analysis! In 2060, artificial intelligence not only reads your purchasing history, but also tracks your preferences, comparing them to millions of other customers. Every click, every pause in front of a product, every simple reaction... turns into valuable information used to create the perfect shopping experience for you. It's as if the store is an old friend who knows you from childhood! This precision in customization makes every visit to the store a unique, personal adventure.

Paragraph 4:

It doesn't just stop at customizing the experience, it goes all the way to predicting the future! Yes, in 2060, the store knows you'll need toothpaste in two days, so it suggests you buy it today at a special price. Or he knows that you are about to travel, so he offers you a smart bag that suits your destination. All these expectations are not magic, but rather intelligence that learns, analyzes, and acts one step ahead of you! It is a world in which technology is intertwined with daily life, to the point where it is difficult to differentiate between human thinking and artificial intelligence.

Paragraph 5:

Marketing analytics in 2060 are like hidden sensors. Companies no longer ask: "What does the customer want?" They ask: "When, where and how do they want it?" These questions are answered by artificial intelligence in moments, using sentiment analysis, tracking behavioral patterns, and reviewing millions of data simultaneously. Companies know when a customer is bored, or when he opens his eyes to a product without deciding to buy it. This depth of understanding gives trade a supernatural power that we have never experienced before.

Paragraph 6:

But the excitement doesn't end here... In 2060, you won't go to the store, the store will come to you! With VR, you will enter a digital world rich in colour, scent and experience. You will wear glasses, and find yourself inside a giant, limitless store, where everything is designed specifically for you. A 3D personal assistant accompanies you, chats with you, and suggests rare pieces that are only visible to you. This experience is like a living technological dream coming true before your eyes.

Paragraph 7:

Development does not stop at the store itself. In 2060, artificial intelligence will be able to design special products just for you! Imagine something in your mind? You tell the system, and in minutes it is manufactured and delivered to you by smart plane! Can a product be born from an idea? In the future, yes. Because trade will not only be buying and selling, but will turn into an interaction between your imagination and technology. It is a revolution in the relationship between man and matter.

Paragraph 8:

Because artificial intelligence is constantly evolving, competition between companies in 2060 will be very fierce. Companies that do not have advanced analysis systems will exit the market. The smartest will survive, not in terms of prices, but in terms of understanding the customer. Small businesses will also benefit from open AI, and will be able to provide personalized services on par with giant corporations. The commercial world will become fairer, but also more demanding of speed and accuracy.

Paragraph 9:

With all this power, the question remains: What about humans? Will his role disappear? The answer is: No. Rather, his role will shift from carrying out tasks, to creating and directing. Humans in 2060 will be the mind that inspires artificial intelligence, feeding it with thoughts, feelings, and goals. AI may be fast, but it doesn't feel. It is the human being who adds the "touch" that cannot be replicated in any program or machine.

Paragraph 10:
Ultimately, AI in commerce in 2060 will not just be a technology, but a way of life. Shopping will turn from a daily need into an amazing experience full of surprises. Technology will be integrated into every step we take inside the store, making every purchase a new adventure. While machines advance, humans will remain the ones steering the rudder and choosing the path. The world of 2060 is not a world of machines, but rather a world of cooperation between artificial intelligence and human intelligence.

Chapter Two: Artificial Intelligence-guided marketing, the role of digital currencies and automatic purchasing 2060

Paragraph 1: Marketing has transformed into a smart digital world
In 2060, all marketing strategies will become incredibly intelligent and directed. Artificial Intelligence will be the brains behind every advertising campaign, controlling the time, place, and person who will see the ad. Companies will no longer need to guess customer needs; Rather, you will know exactly what the customer likes and needs at the same moment. Each ad will be personalized to reflect your own taste, so you'll feel like the brands are speaking to you personally. By tracking every move, every click, and every interaction, AI can tailor advertising messages to each person at the right time.

Paragraph 2: Intelligent analysis of human behavior
Have you ever wondered how companies know you need a particular product before you even realize it? In 2060, artificial intelligence will be able to deeply analyze your digital behavior, by monitoring your interactions on social media platforms, your online search history, and

even your facial expressions via your smartphone camera. All this data will be used to create an advertisement specifically targeted to you, even at the time you prefer, so that every product that appears in front of you is closely related to your actual needs.

Paragraph 3: Digital currencies... the new economy
In 2060, the economy will not be as we know it now. Cryptocurrencies will be the dominant currency, with instant and secure payment systems that enable users to conduct transactions with ease. No need to carry cash or even bank cards; Just a digital wallet on your phone, and purchases are made in moments. These currencies will not be tied to the dollar or euro, but will be completely supported by artificial intelligence. These currencies will replace traditional financial systems, enhancing speed and accuracy in every business transaction.

Paragraph 4: Automatic purchase... with you wherever you are
One of the most important transformations that shopping will witness in 2060 is automatic purchasing. how? Simply put, whenever you need a product, AI will buy it for you. If the system notices that you are constantly using a certain product, it will automatically order it as soon as it runs out. You can even schedule your purchase so that the products are sent to your home or office without you having to take any additional steps. Life will become smoother, and you will never have to worry about running out of essential products.

Paragraph 5: Targeted marketing using augmented reality
Have you ever imagined seeing ads in the world around you? In 2060, targeted ads will appear to you via augmented reality. As soon as you walk into a store, you'll put on smart glasses or lenses, and you'll instantly see offers tailored to you. If you are looking for new shoes, you will be shown details of offers and discounts that suit your taste in shoe

designs. This is not only convenient, it makes shopping more interactive and fun.

Paragraph 6: Personal marketing using artificial intelligence
In the future, there will be no generic advertising, but entirely personal marketing. Imagine that every product that appears in front of you has been selected specifically for you based on your interests, mood and preferences in the moment. This is the future of smart marketing that relies on artificial intelligence to analyze data and use it to benefit the consumer. Companies will be able to reach each customer directly, taking into account their privacy and personal preferences.

Paragraph 7: The role of artificial intelligence in improving advertising campaigns
In 2060, artificial intelligence will be able to optimize advertising campaigns in real time. Instead of waiting weeks to see how effective an advertising campaign is, businesses will be able to see the results of their campaigns in real time. If a campaign is not performing as expected, AI will step in to adjust strategies immediately, helping you reach the right audience and generate more revenue.

Paragraph 8: Digital currencies and their role in reducing costs
Through digital currencies, the costs associated with traditional transactions will be reduced. Think about how to speed up online payments without having to wait for long periods due to banking procedures. Moreover, digital currencies will significantly reduce international remittance costs, boosting global trade and making it easier to conduct business between countries.

Paragraph 9: Integration between artificial intelligence and digital currencies

The integration between artificial intelligence and digital currencies will contribute to achieving a qualitative shift in how commercial transactions are conducted. Artificial intelligence will be responsible for determining the best time and place to execute the transaction via digital currency, taking into account prices and fluctuations in the market. You will have the ability to conduct business transactions more efficiently and securely, in as little as a few seconds.

Paragraph 10: The future of commerce in a fully digital world

With all these amazing developments, the commercial future in 2060 will be a completely digital world, driven by artificial intelligence and digital currencies. Transactions will be faster, more accurate, and more personalized than ever before. Every product will be at your fingertips, and every purchase will be smoother and easier. In the end, shopping will not be just an activity, but rather a rich interactive and digital experience that takes you on a new journey in the world of commerce.

Chapter Two: Inventory Management and Customer Service 2060

With predictions based on reliable sources such as: McKinsey, IBM,) (PwC, Harvard Business Review

---

Paragraph 1: The beginning of the smart inventory revolution

In 2060, store shelves will no longer be filled with chaos or sudden shortages as we see today. Rather, the warehouses will be managed through highly accurate artificial intelligence systems that monitor the movement of products moment by moment. These systems know when a product is running low before it actually happens, and automatically order suppliers for exactly the right amount. According to a McKinsey report, "intelligent inventory forecasting" systems will reduce waste by 80%. and increase response speed by up to 95%

Paragraph 2: Live warehouses

Imagine a warehouse that never sleeps. Its shelves light up when a robot approaches them, and the shelves move toward the employee instead of him moving toward them. This is what a warehouse would look like in 2060. Robots equipped with computer vision and artificial intelligence move at lightning speed between shelves, picking up products, and preparing them for shipping within seconds. Everything works in unseen harmony, yet as precise as a Swiss watch. It is the era of "living warehouses", where no human intervention is needed except for general supervision.

Paragraph 3: Expected, not available, inventory

Artificial intelligence in 2060 will not wait until products run out, but will predict future orders based on purchasing seasons, weather events, and the history of each customer. Will it rain next week? So, the demand for tea and blankets will increase – and the system will act immediately. These predictions are not fantasy, but the result of analyzing billions of data in moments, as IBM futures reports indicate.

Paragraph 4: Goodbye product outage

How many times have you gone to a store and not found what you are looking for? In 2060, this problem will almost disappear. Artificial intelligence will predict when the product will be in demand, and ensure that it reaches the store before it runs out. It will also analyze the behavior of local customers to know what is most popular in each branch. For example, a particular product may be popular in a particular neighborhood but not another, and the branch will be automatically provided with this information, without human intervention.

Paragraph 5: Customer service... but with deep understanding
Have you ever imagined talking to customer service and finding them knowing your problem before you explained it? In 2060, customer service will be managed by intelligent robots, but they won't just be machines that answer questions. She will even understand your tone, your feelings, and even your mood. If you are upset, use a more sympathetic tone. If you're in a hurry, offer a quick solution. According to PwC forecasts, 85% of customer interactions will be automated, but "human-like".completely

---

Paragraph 6: Immediate and personalized responses
Responding to customers in 2060 will not only be fast, but also personalized. The system knows what the customer bought, what his previous problem was, and his preferred means of communication. If the customer likes the video explanation, he will receive a visual explanation. If he prefers to speak directly, a virtual assistant will call him in a natural voice, almost indistinguishable from a human. Everything is done intelligently, respectfully, and quickly.

Paragraph 7: The customer service experience begins before asking
Artificial intelligence will not wait for the customer to complain, but will act before that. If he notices that a purchased product is frequently returned by customers, he will send an alert to management and suggest repair steps. If he sees that the customer has not used the product yet, he will contact him politely, offering help or explanation. It's predictive customer service, one that makes the customer feel important...always.

Paragraph 8: Future customer service employee
Despite the development of artificial intelligence, there will still be a place for humans. But the employee in 2060 will not answer traditional questions. Rather, he will be an "experience manager," supervising the overall performance of smart systems and adding human sensitivity to delicate situations. He will be a creative person, who understands technology and is good at dealing with people. His role will not diminish, but rather it will transform into a more valuable and creative role.

Paragraph 9: Integration between inventory and service
Inventory management and customer service in 2060 will be completely connected. If a customer complains about a product, the sample is immediately withdrawn from the warehouse and examined. If orders for a product increase, the quantity is automatically increased. There is no separation between management and marketing, or between service and inventory. Everything works within one smart network, which monitors, analyses, repairs and develops in real time.

Paragraph 10: A new world of confidence and speed
Ultimately, AI in 2060 will create a more reliable and faster trading experience. The customer knows he will find what he wants, the service will be respectful and efficient, and the products will be managed with unparalleled precision. It is a business that predicts, understands, and serves, without having to wait or complain. It is a world led by intelligence and serving humanity.

Chapter Two: Artificial Intelligence in Industry – Automation in Production Lines

---

!Paragraph 1: Automation starts from here
Imagine entering a factory in the year 2060, and not seeing anyone working on the production lines. Everything is run by intelligent robots that make their own decisions! Manufacturers will no longer need so many workers, because artificial intelligence will be in charge of everything. These robots are able to produce products at the highest speed, highest quality, and with extreme precision, without any human intervention. But how does that happen? Simply put, robots learn from previous experiences and constantly modify themselves to ensure the best performance.

?Paragraph 2: How do intelligent robots help in production
In today's world, we employ people to operate machines and robots in factories. But in 2060, intelligent robots will be able to work on their own. These robots rely on artificial intelligence to understand and analyze every step of production. If part of the process goes wrong, robots will be able to correct errors very quickly before they affect production. For example, if there is a malfunction in a machine, the AI will detect the problem and immediately stop the process to fix it.

Paragraph 3: Extreme precision in manufacturing
Intelligent robots will not only work quickly, but they will also be extremely precise. In the past, there were human errors in manufacturing, but now, artificial intelligence will be able to produce millions of parts with the highest quality and without any glitches. You may see robots assembling small electronic devices or even assembling cars, each part being assembled with great care and exactly as planned.

Section 4: Self-learning robots

One of the most notable features of future automation is that intelligent robots will have the ability to self-learn. The AI will analyze data and past experiences to constantly adjust its performance. For example, if a machine is producing a particular part at a lower speed than expected, the robots will change the settings and make the necessary corrections so that it can achieve the desired efficiency without human intervention. Thus, human errors will be reduced once and for all!

Paragraph 5: How will this affect workers?
Of course, this does not mean that robots will replace all workers in factories, but rather that there will still be an essential role for humans in supervising these robots. Manufacturers will need to monitor the performance of the robots and ensure that everything runs smoothly. In addition, a new type of job will emerge in the future, such as artificial intelligence experts or robot managers who will be responsible for training robots on how to deal with new problems.

Paragraph 6: Reducing costs and increasing efficiency
One of the biggest benefits of automation in factories is reducing costs and increasing production efficiency. In the past, there have been major problems with labor shortages or slow production due to human errors. But with automation, production will become more continuous, and manufacturers will be able to increase production in less time and at lower costs, enhancing the competitiveness of companies.

Paragraph 7: Communication between machines and humans
In the future, human-machine communication will not just be simple conversations, but will be intelligent communication. Robots will be able to talk to humans and receive instructions or even feedback in real time. Have you ever thought about a robot that can talk to you and answer your questions while you monitor the production process? This is the

future that awaits us! This intelligent communication between man and machine will make work more flexible and easier.

Paragraph 8: Sustainable manufacturing
Through automation and artificial intelligence, sustainable manufacturing will be easier to achieve. Intelligent robots can adjust processes to make the most of resources and minimize waste. For example, artificial intelligence will be able to monitor energy consumption at every step of production, which will help companies reduce waste and achieve greater efficiency in the use of materials and energy.

Paragraph 9: From manual labor to artificial intelligence
Do you imagine that a factory that in the past relied on manual labor to produce goods might in the future become an intelligent place where robots work in perfect coordination? By 2060, intelligent machines will be able to adapt to any changes in the production process, making operations more flexible and faster than ever before.

Paragraph 10: What awaits us in the future?
In 2060, automation will become an integral part of every industry, from automobiles to electronics and even the food industry. Artificial intelligence will make it possible for robots to automatically think and adjust themselves according to new data. Everything will be faster, more accurate, and less expensive. With these developments, the industrial world will have unlimited opportunities to achieve sustainable and safe production.

Industrial robots in 2060

Paragraph 1: Robots of the future - friends of factories

In 2060, you will not see factories full of workers as was the case in the past. Instead, it will be smart robots that fill the space! But these robots are not what you know today. They are not just inanimate machines; Rather, they are intelligent robots capable of thinking and making decisions on their own. Like factory friends who work faster and more accurately than any human being. These robots will be able to adapt to any changes that occur in the production lines, making everything run smoothly and incredibly quickly!

Paragraph 2: Robots that learn and develop themselves

In 2060, robots will not only be machines that follow instructions, but will have the ability to self-learn. Imagine that a robot can notice errors or improvements that may occur in the production process, and then adjust itself to improve its performance. If there is a problem with a device or there is a change in materials, the robot can detect this and adjust quickly without human intervention. This ability to learn makes robots more efficient over time.

Paragraph 3: How will humans cooperate with robots?

In the future, humans will no longer work away from robots. Rather, there will be wonderful cooperation between humans and robots. Robots will handle difficult or repetitive tasks, while humans will handle creative or directive tasks. As if there is a team working together to achieve the best results. Think of it as if the robot is your work partner, helping you complete tasks quickly and accurately.

Paragraph 4: Robots that can handle everything

Industrial robots in 2060 will be able to work in difficult or even dangerous environments. You may handle toxic materials or dangerous machinery with ease. It is equipped with advanced sensors that allow it to "see" what is happening around it and make instant decisions based on that. You may find robots diagnosing faults or even performing maintenance during the workflow, which helps keep operations running continuously and without interruption.

Paragraph 5: Smart factories - all automation

Imagine an entire factory working non-stop! In 2060, automation will be at the heart of every manufacturing process. Industrial robots will be responsible for everything: from producing products to packaging and storing them. These robots will collaborate with artificial intelligence systems that monitor the process and adjust it when needed. Everything will happen automatically and quickly, without the need for human intervention in small details.

Paragraph 6: Speed and accuracy in work

Robots in 2060 will be able to operate at unimaginable speeds. It will also be highly accurate, meaning errors will be a thing of the past. For example, if you are in a car factory, robots can fit small parts into the car in an amazing way and with accuracy down to a micrometer. This type of work will not only enhance the quality of the products, but will make production much faster.

Paragraph 7: Preserving the environment using robots

The benefits of robots will not only improve production, but will also help in preserving the environment. Smart robots will be able to monitor energy and resource consumption, contributing to reducing waste. If there is an opportunity to save energy or reduce waste, AI will make the necessary adjustments to achieve greater environmental efficiency, .making factories more sustainable

---

Paragraph 8: Robots that act as experts
In the future, robots will not only have the ability to perform mechanical tasks, but will be like experts in their field. Robots will have the ability to solve problems and come up with innovative solutions using artificial intelligence. If something malfunctions or malfunctions, robots will know exactly how to fix the problem quickly and efficiently without the need .for human intervention

---

Paragraph 9: Providing new jobs for humans
Some may think that robots will completely replace humans in factories, but the opposite is true! As robotics advances, new jobs will emerge in technology. There will be experts to train the robots, managers of intelligent systems, and developers of the technology that runs these robots. People will work more creatively and specialized in a world full of .innovations

---

Paragraph 10: The future awaits us – a world of opportunities
In 2060, we will have a completely new industrial world. Industrial robots will be an essential part of our daily lives. You will be faster, smarter, and more adaptable than ever before. With all these innovations, we will have limitless opportunities to improve production, preserve the environment, and even open the doors to new jobs for humans. The future that awaits .us will be amazing, and robots will be the perfect partner in this future

Failure prediction and quality improvement in 2060

?Paragraph 1: How will fault prediction occur
In 2060, technology will be able to predict breakdowns in factories before they happen! Imagine that an intelligent system in a factory knows exactly when a machine will malfunction. How does that happen? Simply put, using artificial intelligence and big data analysis. Artificial intelligence will constantly monitor machines, learn from their behavior and detect any abnormal changes that may indicate the beginning of a malfunction. This means that it will be able to stop work in time before the malfunction causes bigger problems.

?Paragraph 2: How does artificial intelligence work in predicting faults
Artificial intelligence will be able to analyze historical data of machines in the factory, observing patterns that may indicate a malfunction. For example, if a certain machine starts to operate more slowly or makes unfamiliar sounds, AI can notice these changes and make a prediction that this machine will break down soon. Once this happens, the intelligent system will stop the machine or perform an immediate check to avoid disrupting production.

Paragraph 3: Save time and resources through early forecasting
Predicting failures in 2060 will truly revolutionize the manufacturing industry. Instead of waiting for production to stop due to a sudden malfunction, robots and artificial intelligence systems will analyze data and predict malfunctions before they occur. This will reduce unplanned stops, and make the production process smoother and less expensive. With early analysis, preventative repairs can be made without the need for long downtime.

Paragraph 4: Improving quality thanks to artificial intelligence

Not only breakdowns, but also the quality of products will be improved using AI. how? Simply put, artificial intelligence will monitor every step of production to ensure that every product produced complies with the highest quality standards. If there is any error, such as a small defect in the product or a flaw in the manufacturing process, the AI will immediately detect it and correct it.

Paragraph 5: Machines that constantly monitor quality

In 2060, machines in the factory will be able to monitor quality during manufacturing processes very precisely. It will be equipped with advanced sensors that can verify dimensional accuracy, monitor color, or even examine the texture of products. If any deviation from standards is detected, the machine will stop the process or make an immediate correction. This helps reduce errors and increases customer satisfaction.

Paragraph 6: Prediction of breakdowns at all stages of production

In the future, the ability to predict failures will not be limited to large machines only. Even small equipment or delicate parts of manufacturing systems will be able to alert of malfunctions before they occur. For example, if there is a problem with a small engine or part of the system, AI will predict this before it affects the entire production process. This technology will significantly increase production efficiency.

Paragraph 7: Improving maintenance operations

In 2060, companies will no longer need to perform random routine maintenance as was the case in the past. Instead, the AI will give accurate predictions of when maintenance should be performed based on live data and ongoing analysis. When an upcoming fault is predicted, a notification will be sent to the maintenance team to perform maintenance before the problem occurs. This type of preventive maintenance will contribute to reducing unplanned repair costs.

Paragraph 8: Improving productivity by reducing breakdowns

With fewer unplanned breakdowns and improved preventive maintenance, factories will be able to significantly increase productivity. The machines will operate around the clock without unnecessary stops, allowing for increased production capacity and reduced downtime. Moreover, this will reduce the overall cost of production as manufacturers will not need to spend huge amounts on unplanned repairs.

Paragraph 9: Predicting quality and reducing defects

In the future, AI will go beyond simple failure prediction to include comprehensive quality control. There will be intelligent systems that continuously improve production by monitoring small defects, such as errors in manufacturing or subtle differences in measurements. This will make it easier to detect any problems before they affect the final product, contributing to improved product quality and increased customer satisfaction.

Paragraph 10: A bright future with artificial intelligence

By 2060, AI will be an essential part of every professionally operated factory. From predicting failures to improving quality, AI will provide factories with smarter and more efficient ways to achieve optimal production. Companies will be able to improve their performance and increase their competitiveness on a global level. The future will be full of opportunities, and AI will remain the hidden hero that makes everything better.

Chapter Three: Artificial Intelligence in Agriculture

Smart agriculture and soil analysis

Drones in crop monitoring

Smart irrigation technologies

Paragraph 1: When the earth began to speak

In the year 2060, the Earth is whispering to the farmer what it needs! No more guesswork and no random farming. The soil was planted with precise sensors that send instantaneous signals to a smart system that tells the farmer: "There is a lack of potassium here," or "There is a need for light irrigation." Artificial intelligence has become the earth's ear and tongue, transmitting everything that happens beneath the surface, even in the deepest depths of the roots. It has become possible to care for the soil as if it were a patient whose health condition we monitor at every moment.

Paragraph 2: Farms that think and plan

Can you imagine a farm that knows when it will rain, and plans the planting process weeks in advance? This is the reality of smart agriculture. Artificial intelligence systems predict weather conditions, analyze soil components, and then draw up an integrated agricultural plan: What do we plant? when? And how? No more random decisions. The farmer became like a military commander, leading an army of intelligent machines, and every step was carefully and calmly thought out.

Paragraph 3: Eyes in the sky... and minds under the dirt

In the sky, drones equipped with thermal cameras and optical analyzers fly, monitoring the health of plants by the color of their leaves. Underground, smart sensors sense the soil's temperature, moisture, and chemical composition. All this data is sent directly to a central system, like the farm's superbrain. In seconds, the state of every inch of the field is mapped and intelligent commands are executed.

Paragraph 4: Intelligence is diagnosed before the disaster strikes
One of the biggest achievements of artificial intelligence in agriculture: predicting problems before they happen. The smart system can detect the beginning of a plant disease from just a slight difference in leaf color! Sends early warning and suggests treatment. In the past, fields were destroyed before the farmer noticed what was happening, but today, every plant is monitored as if it were a patient in the care room, and every warning saves a crop.

Paragraph 5: Soil is no longer a mystery
In the past, soil was checked manually perhaps once a season. Now, AI performs hundreds of analyzes every day! It knows the levels of nitrogen, phosphorus, and calcium accurately, and follows up on real-time changes. Based on this data, the system determines the ideal timing for planting, fertilizing or plowing. Soil is no longer a mystery, but an open book that technology can easily read.

Paragraph 6: Agriculture without waste... not a drop of water wasted
In 2060, every drop of water is precisely counted. Artificial intelligence decides when, where and how to water plants, and prevents excessive or unnecessary watering. The smart irrigation system nourishes the plant according to its need, and distributes water using drip or automatic spraying technology. This precise control has saved millions

of liters of water, increased crop production, and dramatically reduced
costs.

Paragraph 7: The planting season begins from the computer
The farmer no longer waits for the "season" as before. Using artificial
intelligence, weather, soil and market data are analyzed, and the best
planting time is determined with scientific precision. The system
suggests: "Plant tomatoes next week, as the humidity is appropriate and
the markets demand it." It's a programmed planting season, driven by
science, that minimizes risk and maximizes profits.

Paragraph 8: AI teaches the farmer
In 2060, the farmer is no longer alone in his decisions. Whenever
something unexpected happens, the system sends a voice or written
recommendation to its mobile device: "Add biofertilizer today," or "Be
careful not to increase salinity." These tips are backed by real-time
research and data. The farmer learns from the machine and becomes an
expert thanks to it. A new relationship of intelligent cooperation between
human and technology.

Paragraph 9: More crops...higher quality
Thanks to artificial intelligence, success is not only about quantity, but
also about quality. Every grain of fruit, and every ear of wheat, emerges
complete in form and taste. Because the system monitors nutrition,
precisely adjusts growing conditions, and prevents diseases before they
start. Crops have become luxurious, suitable for export and global
competition. This is the agriculture of the future...an unmistakable
agriculture.

Paragraph 10: Agriculture in 2060... the dream has become a reality

In the past, farming was stressful and uncertain. In 2060, smart agriculture has become a model of creativity and integration between humans and machines. Artificial intelligence makes the farmer produce more, consume less, and protect the environment. From grain to harvest, everything is managed with precision and calm. The Earth has become technology-friendly, and the future is green like never before.

--Drones in crop monitoring

Paragraph 1: Heaven watches the Earth carefully

In 2060, monitoring fields no longer requires walking under the sun or manually checking each plant. A small drone, the size of the palm of a hand, flies quietly over the farm, like a magic eye that sees every detail. It analyzes photos of plants from above, notes leaf color, and detects early signs of any disease or nutritional deficiency. Within minutes, she sends an accurate report to the farmer's phone: "Watch out! There are signs of wilting in the northern corner." Speed, precision, and quiet... these are the qualities of the new crop monitor.

Paragraph 2: Intelligence in two wings

These planes are not just flying machines, but flying minds. It is equipped with thermal cameras, smart sensors, and real-time image analysis software. She doesn't just see plants, she understands them. You know when a plant needs water, when it has been attacked by an insect, and you can even differentiate between two types of diseases based on the shape of the spot on the leaf! In the sky, there is an electronic agricultural doctor who monitors the crops better than any human.

Paragraph 3: Speed that saves the crop

In agriculture, time means life. Before 2060, a farmer would have discovered a disease within days of its spread. Today, the drone detects the problem on the same day, and sometimes at the same hour. This early detection saves the crop from loss and reduces the need for chemicals. Instead of spraying the entire field, the drone directs the treatment only to the affected area. Faster, cleaner, smarter.

Paragraph 4: The eye that never sleeps

Drones operate day and night. In the dark, they use night cameras and thermal rays that see the heat given off by plants. If one plant overheats in the middle of an entire field, you know something is wrong. It is as if there is an intelligent being in the sky, who never sleeps or gets tired, watching every inch of the earth with an expert eye. These drones have become loyal friends to farmers, protecting them from losses and helping them succeed.

Paragraph 5: Airplanes create a green revolution

In 2060, agriculture is no longer just about seedlings, watering, and plowing. Rather, it has become a high-tech field, involving aircraft, artificial intelligence, and big data. Drones have truly revolutionized the way of farming, making the farmer produce more, lose less, and deal with his land more precisely. It is a green revolution that begins from the sky... and ends with abundant fruits and high quality.

Smart irrigation technologies
Smart irrigation technologies in 2060:

Paragraph 1: When the plant speaks... and intelligence hears it

In the year 2060, it is no longer the farmer who decides when to irrigate his crops, but rather the plants themselves send electronic signals that are translated by intelligent systems connected to sensors buried in the soil. These sensors monitor soil moisture, temperature, nutrient composition, and even biological activity below the surface. When the soil needs water, the device not only sends an alarm, but immediately begins pumping water into drip or sprinkler irrigation systems, and distributes it to the plant in a specific amount, neither more nor less. Artificial intelligence does not irrigate the entire field, but only the place where it is needed, and in the quantity each plant needs! Not only that, but the system monitors the weather: if there is rain expected after two hours, it automatically postpones watering to save water. If the soil in a certain part is still wet from yesterday, do not water it again. It is an intelligent system that works silently, precisely, and with maximum efficiency, so much so that the farmer says: "I don't irrigate... I just watch, and the artificial intelligence does the rest".

Paragraph 2: Water drops are under the control of the electronic mind
In the past, farms were uncontrollably flooded with water, which harmed crops and soil. In 2060, the situation is completely different. Every drop of water is calculated and distributed based on precise equations, controlled by an intelligent irrigation system that resembles an "electronic brain." This system does not pump water randomly, but rather checks the condition of each plant, and decides the required amount in minutes and milliliters. Imagine that this system is connected to satellites and weather devices, so it knows if the day is very hot, or if the humidity is high, and adjusts the irrigation schedule automatically. The farmer no longer carries a water hose, but a small tablet, which shows him a map of the ground moisture at every corner, giving him complete control from the monitoring room or even from his home.

Paragraph 3: Irrigation according to the biological temperament of the plants
In 2060, every plant is treated as a sentient creature with its own temperament. The smart system does not irrigate all plants in the same way, but rather it recognizes the type of crop, its age, and the extent of

its water absorption, and adjusts the irrigation pattern accordingly. Tomato plants are different from wheat, and wheat is different from grapes. Over time, the AI learns how each plant responds to irrigation, and adjusts the watering schedule personally for each part of the field! It is as if each plant has its own "medical file". This precision made crops grow healthier, and diseases caused by excess moisture or drought were reduced.

Paragraph 4: Smart irrigation saves the planet

The benefits of smart irrigation do not stop at the farm borders, but extend to protecting the environment and the planet. In 2060, water conservation has become a global priority, with water resources becoming scarce in many regions. Smart irrigation systems have helped reduce water consumption by up to 70%, compared to traditional methods. It also prevented the leakage of excess water, which carried fertilizers into the rivers and polluted the environment. Smart irrigation has become a smart environmental solution that combines abundant production and the preservation of natural resources, as if the earth and humans were working together in complete harmony.

Paragraph 5: Agriculture has become a game of intelligence

In the year 2060, the farmer is no longer just a man working with his hands, but a skilled engineer managing an intelligent system of algorithms, sensors, and small aircraft. Smart irrigation techniques have made agriculture a game of intelligence and creativity, where the farmer monitors his land like a pilot monitors an airplane screen. He distributes water exactly as he needs it, protects each seedling from thirst, and monitors the data that appears in front of him moment by moment. The farm is no longer silent, but speaks with numbers and graphs, and the farmer reads them and interacts with them. It is a new, fun, exciting world, and the most beautiful thing is that it preserves everything: plants, water, and the environment.

Chapter Four: Artificial Intelligence in Tourism

,Chapter Four: Artificial Intelligence in Tourism - Digital Tour Guide 2060
With a focus on visiting archaeological monuments using artificial
:intelligence techniques

Paragraph 1: A journey in time with a smart voice and a digital face
In the year 2060, tourists no longer need to carry maps or memorize the
names of landmarks, because the tour guide has become smart and
alive, living in your phone, your watch, or even in your smart lenses. As
soon as you step inside an archaeological site, the system automatically
recognizes you and begins designing a personalized tour for you. If you
are a fan of the Pharaohs, he takes you on a 3D tour inside
Tutankhamun's tomb, and shows you the details of daily life in ancient
Egypt as if you are watching a live movie, but you are inside it! If you are
standing in front of a broken statue or a collapsed wall, the guide shows
you the original form thousands of years ago, with a soft voiceover
explaining the history in simple and heart-felt language. This guide
speaks your language, knows your interests, and suggests places you
didn't know existed. He can even book you a ticket to the next museum,
or tell you where the nearest café is to take a break. He is not just a
guide, but an intelligent travel companion, who lives with you every
moment, and turns every visit into a charming cognitive adventure,
mixed with excitement, amazement, and nostalgia for a past that you did
.not live, but which pulses before you in all its details

Paragraph 2: Every trace has a story... and intelligence tells it to you

In the year 2060, artificial intelligence is able to collect millions of stories and information from history books and archaeological research, and present them to you in a charming, personal style. As you walk between the columns of Karnak or the statues of the Temple of Abu Simbel, your intelligent guide tells you that these columns were lit by fire at night, and that the priests walked in silence between their walls during rituals. You can even choose the style of explanation: Do you prefer dramatic narration? Or a scientific method? Or a story directed at children? With one click everything changes! And you begin to see the scene as if you were inside it: colors, costumes, sounds, and even ancient smells can be simulated using augmented reality technology and artificial intelligence. The monument is no longer just silent stones, but has become a living theater, taking you back thousands of years, and the guide is the intelligent narrator who takes your hand in every moment.

Paragraph 3: From the pyramid to the Tower of Babel in minutes

In 2060, moving between archaeological sites is no longer as stressful as in the past. Using a smart guide, you can tour the pyramids in the morning, then visit the ruins of Babylon in the evening, without moving from your place! "Instant Smart Tours" technology allows you to enter an archaeological site digitally using virtual reality glasses, and experience the full feeling of walking through it, contemplating inscriptions, touching virtual walls, and even interacting with historical figures simulated by artificial intelligence. You can ask the guide: "Why was this temple built?" He will answer you in a clear voice, and show you an interactive clip explaining the reason, supported by historical sources. It is the joy of travel, knowledge, and live experience, without the need to book planes or travel thousands of kilometers. Tourism has become closer...and deeper!

Paragraph 4: Your personal companion who knows you better than yourself

The intelligent guide in 2060 not only provides information, but also learns from you and adapts with you. If he notices that you're spending more time looking at inscriptions, he'll suggest symbol-rich temples. If you show interest in Greek civilization, Greek sites and documentaries will be included for you during your break. This guide is not static, but rather develops itself daily by analyzing your preferences, and even your facial expressions or the tone of your voice if you are tired or excited. Imagine that when you visit an archaeological site in Alexandria, it reminds you that your grandfather visited this place before - if it is registered in your family's digital record - and displays old photos of him there! The guide has become a loyal friend, a second eye that sees beyond the stone, and reveals to you the layers of history from your perspective, not from the perspective of a static book.

Paragraph 5: Intelligence creates an unforgettable experience
Tourism is no longer just quick pictures in front of silent monuments, but has become an integrated personal experience, fraught with amazement, feelings, and knowledge. Artificial intelligence in 2060 makes every trip a story to tell, and every visit an unforgettable moment. Imagine that after completing your visit, you receive a memorial video prepared by the smart guide, collecting your moments, photos, comments, and even the music you chose during the tour. It even recommends your next trip based on what you liked! Did you like the arts? So your next trip to Rome. Are you fascinated by temples? So get ready to visit India. It is intelligent, colorful and exciting tourism, where every step turns into an adventure, every piece of information into a magical moment, and every stone into a story waiting to be discovered.

Smart trip planning 2060
Artificial intelligence in trip planning in 2060, and the possible side effects of this development, such as over-reliance, loss of the sense of real surprises, and isolation:

Paragraph 1: Amazing comfort... but it hides a lot!
In 2060, when trips are planned using artificial intelligence, everything seems perfect. No delay, no fatigue, and no thinking. Just a trip designed

just for you. But behind this amazing comfort, there are side effects that many do not feel. Complete reliance on intelligence makes some people lose their sense of adventure. She no longer searches or imagines, and she no longer asks others or miscalculates. Everything is guaranteed... and this might kill part of the beauty of travel: the real surprises. Some travelers are beginning to feel that trips are like an "improved version of their dreams," but without that spontaneous feeling that makes a moment of getting lost, or discovering a restaurant by chance, unforgettable.

Paragraph 2: The flight is under constant monitoring
In 2060, you are never alone anymore. Throughout the journey, the artificial intelligence monitors your pulse, movement, and even emotions. This monitoring is meant to serve you, but it begs the question: Are you still completely free? Some travelers felt that having this "invisible companion" all the time made them unable to act spontaneously. Can you cry into the sunset without being shown a soothing video? Or to laugh at a random situation without the intervention of intelligence by suggesting an entertaining post? This clever experiment may rob you of a part of the "human moment," where every feeling turns into information, and every reaction into an algorithm.

Paragraph 3: Intelligence directs the journey... and you watch
Smart planning is great, but in some cases, the traveler becomes just a passenger on a journey in which he has no real decision to make. The schedule changes without asking, recommendations are constantly displayed, and suggestions are implemented automatically. This makes some people feel like they are watching their lives from the outside. The Journey turned out to be a great movie...but it's not directed by you. Will this lead to a loss of planning skills in the future? Will a person lose the ability to make simple decisions such as "Where do I go? When? And with whom?" It's great for the trip to be perfect, but it's even more wonderful for you to be a part of creating it.

Paragraph 4: Intelligence knows you more than you know yourself
This may seem convenient, even impressive: for the system to know your preferred destination even before you tell it, to suggest an activity that suits your psychological state before you know it. But...what if you start to feel that intelligence is controlling your choices? What if you thought you made the choice yourself, while he was the one who planted the idea in your mind? In 2060, artificial intelligence doesn't just do the job, it may influence your tastes and decisions. You may think you like a city, when in fact you were directed there because your data says so. Will humans still have true freedom to experience new things, or will we continue to live only within what the algorithms expect?

Paragraph 5: Pleasure in the unknown... does it still exist?
One of the most beautiful moments of travel throughout history is the moment of getting lost, a random discovery, or even a breakdown that later becomes a joke. But with AI in 2060, everything is predictable, calculated, and controlled. There is no error, and no opportunity for spontaneous experimentation. This is what makes some people feel that the fun has disappeared from the heart of the trip. The trips have become beautiful... but too "clean". Without the small challenges, without the strange surprises, does the journey have any soul left? This is the new ethical challenge: how do we preserve the magic of travel, while harnessing the power of artificial intelligence?

Simultaneous interpretation and the personal tourist experience in 2060

Paragraph 1: The language of the world... is no longer a barrier
In 2060, tourists no longer need to learn the languages of the countries they visit. It is enough for him to wear a small earphone, or put a smart

lens on his eye, to have everything he hears and sees translated instantly! Imagine that you are in the heart of a popular market in Tokyo, hearing the vendors speaking Japanese, but in your ear... you hear Arabic! Don't wait for a translation, don't look for a dictionary, just speak your language and everyone will understand you. Even road signs are translated instantly in front of you on your smart glasses. It is a new freedom that ignites the passion for travel and opens the doors of the world without borders, so that every country seems to speak to you in the language of your heart.

Paragraph 2: Every tourist has his own world

In 2060, journeys are no longer uniform for everyone. Every tourist lives a personal experience designed just for him, according to his interests, psychological state, and even his memory! Artificial intelligence accompanies you like a close friend, knowing that you love art, taking you to hidden galleries that only locals know about. And if you love food, he leads you to a popular chef in an old alley who will make you a dish that will remain in your memory forever. No traditional schedules, no boring group trips. It is an adventure that resembles you, and grows with you, as if the whole city revolves around you and addresses you alone.

Paragraph 3: Talking to strangers has become fun

How many times have you traveled and wished you could talk to an old lady in a remote village? Or to understand the story of a bookseller in Paris? In 2060, artificial intelligence will realize this dream. You pick up your phone or just look through your glasses and start a real, natural, lag-free conversation with anyone in any language. The laugh is translated, the joke is understood, and even popular proverbs are smoothly interpreted. This made the world more humane and closer to the heart. Language is no longer a barrier, but a bridge, carrying stories from one continent to another, making every conversation a warm adventure.

Paragraph 4: Your moments... are told to you again
In the future, you don't just live in the moment, but it is recreated for you in a way that surprises you. Imagine that you are walking on an ancient street in Rome, and suddenly the artificial intelligence tells you about a battle that took place here 500 years ago, with cinematic sound and visual effects that make you see what happened as if you were there! Every moment holds a story, and every stone under your feet speaks a history. Translation is not only for people's language, but also for time and place. It is a rich experience that turns every minute of your trip into an exciting movie, with you as the hero in it.

Paragraph 5: The other side of comfort
Despite this beauty, there is a hidden side. In some moments, the tourist forgets to live the moment with its spontaneity. Automatic translation may make you lose the joy of trying, and the nice details of mistakes. Intelligent personal experience may make everything so perfect that you feel that you are not discovering something for yourself, but that it is being discovered for you. Here the challenge arises: how do we balance comfort and surprise? Between technology and spontaneity? But even so, there is no doubt that travel in 2060 will become more beautiful, smarter, and more soulful. It is a new era of travel... where there is no stranger, and no place is far from you.

Chapter Six: Artificial Intelligence in Aviation

Self-driving aircraft

Improving navigation and safety systems

—Air traffic management and control centers

Chapter Six: Artificial Intelligence in Aviation - Self-Driving Aircraft 2060

Paragraph 1: A new beginning in the future sky

In the year 2060, airplanes are no longer just means of transportation, but technical masterpieces that float in the sky without human pilots. Self-driving planes are equipped with advanced artificial intelligence that controls everything with incredible precision, from take-off to landing. You enter the airport, board the plane, sit down, and begin the flight... without seeing a pilot in the cockpit! Intelligence tracks weather conditions, adjusts balance, and automatically changes course if an emergency occurs. People were initially worried, but after millions of successful flights, these planes became a symbol of comfort and safety, and even a means of transporting dreams towards a world free of human error.

Paragraph 2: Goodbye human errors

One of the most notable benefits brought by self-driving aircraft is that they have dramatically reduced accidents. In the past, human error was the cause of many disasters, but in 2060, algorithms do not forget, do not get tired, and do not get distracted. AI studies millions of previous flights every moment, and learns from them in real time, making it more accurate than any human pilot. Even if the plane enters a sudden storm, it acts extremely quickly, rebalancing and changing course within a fraction of a second. It's a calm drive, no tension, no hesitation, just a fluidity that dazzles you and gives you confidence that the sky is no longer a danger.

Paragraph 3: Passenger experience... worry-free

Can you imagine traveling on a plane without seeing a pilot? At first it seems strange, but in 2060, this idea became normal. Passengers sit in their seats and talk to the aircraft's intelligent assistant via a screen or voice. "When do we arrive?", "Are there turbulence?", "Can I postpone my meal?"... Everything is done with a touch or voice command. Some feel more comfortable because they know that the plane is controlled by precise digital minds, unaffected by psychological pressure or fatigue. All information is available moment by moment, making passengers feel that they are on a transparent and safe journey more than ever before.

Paragraph 4: Will the pilot profession disappear?

Here the big question arises: Are pilots out of a role? In 2060, the profession of pilot has not been completely abolished, but it has changed. The pilot is now a "technical supervisor" of the systems, monitoring the AI and intervening only in extreme cases. This role is less stressful, but requires different skills, closer to engineering than aviation. Some see this as a natural development, others feel sad because the profession of a pilot was a symbol of courage and discipline. Artificial intelligence has not completely eliminated humans, but it has turned them into an observer in a world governed by machines, with precision and agility... but also with a new kind of ambiguity.

Paragraph 5: The future still flies!

Flights in 2060 will be faster, safer, and less expensive thanks to self-driving planes. But the most beautiful question: Where will the future take us next? There are experiments on planes without windows, showing you digital panoramic views from inside that mimic nature. There are solar-powered planes that fly thousands of kilometers non-stop. Some of them can adapt to the passengers' feelings, changing the lighting, music, and even the degree of vibration according to the psychological state. We are not only experiencing a revolution in transportation, but we stand before a new door of flying sensation... where every trip becomes a unique experience that tells an unforgettable story.

Improving navigation and safety systems 2060

Paragraph 1: Flying with an eye that never sleeps
In 2060, air navigation systems are no longer as we knew them. Airplanes now have an "intelligent mind" that sees everything around them in the sky and on the ground, even before danger appears! Traditional radars have evolved into intelligent systems based on artificial intelligence, which predict climate changes and analyze air traffic every second. If there's danger coming — like an approaching plane or an unexpected storm — she makes decisions at lightning speed, adjusting course before passengers feel any anxiety. It's not just a plane flying, but an intelligent being that protects itself and you in amazing silence.

Paragraph 2: A navigation network that talks to each other
Imagine that all planes around the world were now "talking" to each other in a precise digital language! In the year 2060, aircraft, airports, satellites and ground systems are all connected to a single network, managing air navigation like an intelligent chess game. Every step is calculated, and every path is monitored moment by moment. If the weather changes over a particular country, all aircraft in the air receive an immediate alert. This network never sleeps, nor does it neglect, making flying safer and more organized than ever before. It is a silent revolution that made the sky a safe space like the room in your home.

Paragraph 3: Safety is not only in emergencies
In 2060, the concept of aviation safety is no longer limited to emergency situations only. The plane now "feels" the state of every part of it. From engines to airplane wings, there are tiny sensors that monitor performance and send continuous signals to an intelligent system that reads and compares them with billions of previous data. If it notices a minor defect that might develop, it gives an immediate alert, and the problem is fixed before it starts. Even the passengers themselves have become part of this system, as the seats monitor health indicators and

alert the crew if one of them feels tired or has a health problem. Safety
here is not a reaction, but a way of life.

Paragraph 4: Training artificial intelligence on human errors
The artificial intelligence that manages navigation and safety in aviation
learns not only from good data, but also from mistakes. In 2060, every
incident or defect in the world is transformed into an intelligent lesson,
entered into the artificial navigation memory to avoid it in the future.
This means that the plane becomes "smarter" with each new flight. They
are constantly learning and improving, becoming more sensitive to
potential threats. The more experiments there are, the more precise the
systems become, leaving us flying in an environment that evolves faster
than any danger could arise.

Paragraph 5: When safety becomes part of the fun
Safety may always seem like a serious and heavy topic, but in 2060 it
has become part of the travel experience itself. In modern aircraft,
screens show you real-time navigation data and make you feel like you
are "piloting" the flight alongside the artificial intelligence. Every
passenger has access to the route, speed, weather changes, and even
engine performance! This transparency gives the traveler a feeling of
security and confidence, and even turns him into part of the smart,
technological journey. Safety has become attractive, simple, and
cheerful... making you feel that the future is not only safer, but more
exciting.

Air traffic management and control centers 2060

Paragraph 1: A crowded sky... and an intelligent mind managing it

In the year 2060, the sky is no longer a random arena filled with planes from every direction. Rather, it has become a tight system managed by a superhuman artificial intelligence that controls the movement of hundreds of thousands of aircraft at the same time. This central brain knows when each plane takes off, where it is headed, and how much time and space it needs in the air. Imagine that you are watching a giant beehive, but each bee (flying) moves with incredible precision, does not collide, and is not delayed. Coordination between air navigation and control centers has become global, as if the entire world has become a single control tower pulsing with smart signals.

…Paragraph 2: Control centers without humans? Yes but In the 2060s, air control centers went from rooms full of humans to environments that relied primarily on artificial intelligence. The aeronautical engineer no longer monitors each plane himself, but rather "trains" the artificial intelligence on how to make decisions, and supervises it from afar. Smart programs analyze millions of data every second: weather, crowding, emergencies, and even the psychological state of some human pilots, if they exist! However, the role of the human has not been completely abolished, but has become more focused and professional, intervening only in extreme cases, while leaving the finer details to the machine mind.

Paragraph 3: The system knows you before you arrive In the future, once your aircraft takes off, it will become a "known part" of the intelligent flight management network. The plane transmits its position, speed, and heading to hundreds of stations around the world, and each control center prepares to receive it and pass it before it approaches. This hidden coordination prevents any congestion in the airways, and gives the plane the freedom to move quickly and smoothly. If any disruption occurs in the air, all affected aircraft are automatically notified. Everything is connected, alert, as if the sky has become a "huge Wi-Fi network" from which nothing escapes.

Paragraph 4: From warning to expectation

Modern systems in 2060 do not wait for danger to occur in order to take action, but rather anticipate it before it occurs. If it notices expected congestion at a particular airport, it automatically adjusts routes and notifies control centers and aircraft of the change. If a storm approaches, the flight altitude and landing time are changed before passengers feel any turbulence. This type of predictive navigation greatly reduced delays and risks, and made flying more precise and quiet. Artificial intelligence now thinks like expert pilots... but faster, quieter, and more precise.

Paragraph 5: Beyond the glass towers

Control centers are no longer just those tall glass towers at airports. In 2060, there are virtual centers operating remotely, from other countries or from secret locations, that manage air navigation anywhere in the world. Everything is based on live data and instant communication, allowing tasks to be distributed and stress reduced. Even in times of crisis, a center in Japan can manage the airspace of a country in Africa within seconds, and vice versa. This flexibility has made aviation resistant to disasters, and more prepared for any circumstance, as if the entire Earth is working as one mind to ensure a safe journey for every person in the sky.

Chapter Seven: Artificial Intelligence in Maritime Transport
Intelligent ships and automated steering

Weather forecasting techniques and trajectories

Maritime security and global trade

Chapter Seven: Artificial Intelligence in Maritime Transport – Smart Ships and Automated Steering 2060

?Paragraph 1: A sea without a captain
In the year 2060, giant ships no longer need a captain holding the helm with his hands. Smart ships have become dependent on automated guidance systems powered by artificial intelligence, navigating the oceans with high precision and without direct human intervention. From the moment of take-off to the moment of arrival, the ship knows its position, its course, and even the weather it will encounter hundreds of miles away. It avoids storms, locates the quickest routes, and is surprisingly fuel efficient. Some call them "digital whales," because they swim quietly and confidently in the middle of the ocean, guiding themselves without the need for anyone to shout into the microphone or monitor the radar day or night.

Paragraph 2: Intelligent steering... flawless
Smart ships in 2060 will be equipped with navigation systems that can read digital marine charts and analyze them in real time. She doesn't just see the sea, she understands it. Know the currents, depths, and hidden reefs. If another ship appears kilometers away, it analyzes its speed and direction, and redraws the course in a split second to avoid a collision. This automated routing is managed through a network connected to satellites and data centers around the world. Every ship at sea is constantly sending and receiving information, as if participating in a global conversation about the state of the sea and its dangers.

Paragraph 3: A small crew and smart tasks
With artificial intelligence, ships no longer need dozens of sailors as in the past. A small crew is enough to monitor the systems, because most tasks have become automated: from steering, to starting the engines, to checking the cargo. Even the crew itself gets intelligent assistance, such as robots that perform inspections, and drones that monitor the sea surface from the air. Everything has become easier, more precise, and less risky. Some even predict that future ships will sail from port to port

without anyone on board, only through artificial intelligence and remote monitoring.

Paragraph 4: Safety first... intelligence second
Safety in maritime transport has greatly improved thanks to artificial intelligence. Smart ships can predict malfunctions before they occur and automatically send alerts to maintenance centers. If a leak or fire occurs, the systems quickly seal off and isolate the affected areas, preventing disaster before it begins. It can also summon rescue aircraft or communicate with the nearest ship within moments. Artificial intelligence here not only protects goods, but also lives, and makes the sea, which was once a symbol of danger and mystery, a safer and more balanced space.

Paragraph 5: The future of maritime trade is in the grip of intelligence
Thanks to smart ships, the map of global trade has changed. Travel has become faster, less expensive, and more organized. The ports of the future are equipped with smart systems that receive ships and unload containers automatically, without waiting or congestion. Every ship knows precisely the time of its entry and exit, and calculates the amounts of fuel required and the cost of the trip, moment by moment. This not only reduces expenses, but also reduces environmental impact, because smart ships choose routes that consume the least fuel and produce the least pollution. Artificial intelligence has not only made the sea smarter, but greener and more humane.

Weather forecasting and routing techniques 2060 in maritime transport

---

Paragraph 1: The weather is no longer a surprise
In the past, weather changes at sea were a great danger and could lead to disasters. In the year 2060, thanks to artificial intelligence, the weather

is no longer a surprise! Smart ships rely on advanced systems that collect data from satellites, marine buoys, and connected sensors around the world. These systems monitor atmospheric pressure, currents, and temperatures, and analyze them in real time to provide very accurate forecasts. The ship knows many hours in advance when the storm will begin, and how severe it will be, and chooses an alternative course smoothly, as if it is reading the future.

Paragraph 2: Smart routes save lives

In 2060, ships no longer just follow traditional routes, they make their own way! Intelligent routing systems integrate weather data, wave movement, wind speed, and even marine traffic information, to determine the best route at every moment. If there is a sudden weather disturbance or the appearance of a distant hurricane, the ship immediately recalculates its course and changes direction. This flexibility not only maintains speed of access, but also protects lives and prevents losses. It is an intelligence that interacts with nature and makes it a friend instead of an enemy.

Paragraph 3: ShA universal cry that sees everything

Imagine that all the world's oceans were connected to a single network that monitored the weather and water real-time. In 2060, there is a global system called the Eye of the Sea, collecting data from hundreds of satellites, seaplanes, and floating robots. This system sends instant reports to ships about the sea state at every point they pass. Even in the farthest oceans, ships do not move blindly, but rather with intelligent eyes that monitor every incoming wave and every cloud in the sky, as if they are moving under the care of a digital angel that never sleeps.

Paragraph 4: Accurate predictions by the second

What sets weather technologies apart in 2060 is their astonishing accuracy. Forecasts are no longer in days or hours, but in minutes and seconds. The ship knows when the wind will blow, when it will ease, and when it will change. This allows it to control speed, and choose precise sailing time to avoid delays or violent tremors. Even ports receive this data in advance, preparing reception based on sea conditions. It is an

intelligent communication between sky, sea and people, making maritime
transportation safer, more streamlined and more enjoyable.

Paragraph 5: Artificial intelligence learns from the sea
Systems in 2060 don't just monitor the weather, they learn from it. Every voyage,
every sea change, is recorded in a giant database. Artificial intelligence analyzes this
data and learns from it to become more accurate in the future. This ability to learn
made ships treat the sea as if it were an old friend. No fear of storms and no worry of
surprises, because intelligence is improving day by day, making every sea voyage
calmer, safer and smarter.

Maritime Security and Global Trade 2060

Paragraph 1: The sea is no longer the land of thieves
In the past, sea trade was always threatened by piracy and smuggling, but in 2060, the
rules have completely changed. Artificial intelligence has become a vigilant sentinel
for every ship, detecting strange movements and raising immediate alerts of any
danger. Thermal cameras, drones, and smart radars monitor every corner of the ship
and its surrounding ocean. If a suspicious boat approaches, the system recognizes it
before it poses a danger and notifies the nearest maritime authorities. It is a new era...
the sea is guarded by intelligence, not just by weapons.

Paragraph 2: A globally connected maritime security network
Every ship in 2060 is connected to a global security network known as the Ocean
Shield, a massive artificial intelligence system that monitors every movement on the
high seas. If a threat is detected anywhere in the world, nearby ships are notified
within seconds. Ports also interact directly with this network, closing or securing its
entrances if necessary. This network not only monitors, but learns from every
incident, anticipating attacks before they happen. Even the pirates themselves
became afraid of it, because the chances of escape became almost impossible.

Paragraph 3: Global trade is faster and safer
Smart maritime security not only protects ships, but also accelerates global trade. In
2060, shipments arrive in record times, without delays due to random inspections or
accidents. Artificial intelligence digitally sorts shipments and analyzes their contents,
detecting contraband by analyzing container data before they are even opened. Each

container carries a digital fingerprint, tracking its journey from source to consumer. This means complete transparency and supply chains that are not easily compromised.

Paragraph 4: Combating smuggling and piracy with intelligence
There was no longer any need for chases at sea. In 2060, smuggling is tackled in a different way: data analysis and prediction. Artificial intelligence studies ship movements and detects strange patterns that indicate illegal activity. Did the ship suddenly change course? Did you turn off its signals? Are you standing in a suspicious place? This is immediately monitored, and surveillance aircraft or ships are directed to quickly intervene in the area. Even concealment is no longer useful, because the sea has become exposed to intelligent eyes that never sleep.

Paragraph 5: The future of trade without fear
Maritime security in 2060 will make trade between countries more prosperous and confident. Countries no longer fear losing their shipments, or paying exorbitant insurance due to risks. Even small companies can easily enter the global trade market, because the cost, time and risks have decreased. Smart security has opened new doors for growth, creating jobs and business areas that did not exist before. The sea, once a battlefield, is today a secure digital route carrying goods and dreams from continent to continent.

Chapter Eight: Artificial Intelligence in the Military Field

Smart weapons and drones

Battlefield analysis and decision making

Cyber defenses and espionage

Chapter Eight: Artificial Intelligence in the Military Field - Smart Weapons and Drones
2060

Paragraph 1: Smart weapons...a huge leap in military power
In the year 2060, smart weapons have become more advanced than anyone could have imagined. These weapons not only need power, but also rely on artificial intelligence to analyze the battle and identify targets with amazing accuracy. From cannons that select the most important targets to missiles that travel across the sky

targeting enemy vehicles, battle has become more precise and smarter. Smart weapons do not require emotional or human decisions under pressure, but rather make completely autonomous decisions based on a graphical analysis of threats. In the future, soldiers may not need to worry about random attacks, because artificial intelligence will be the commander of the battle.

Paragraph 2: Drones... the eye of the sky that never ignores
Imagine that there are drones in the sky all the time, never stopping or sleeping, monitoring all the enemy's movements and collecting vital information moment by moment. In 2060, drones have become an essential part of military strategy. Its mission is not only limited to gathering intelligence, but it can also carry out attacks with complete precision. Thanks to artificial intelligence, drones can identify precise targets anywhere, and destroy them quickly and without error. It can also make autonomous decisions based on the current situation on the ground, reducing the need for human intervention and increasing the effectiveness of attacks.

Paragraph 3: Artificial intelligence in future wars
Future wars will not just be conflicts between armies, but will be a race between intelligent systems. Drones, smart weapons, and AI-powered military robots will completely change the way armies conduct their battles. These systems are incredibly capable of interacting with each other, coordinating attacks and defenses. Such systems can determine the enemy's location in seconds, and determine the best strategy for dealing with complex situations in record time. Artificial intelligence is not only in the equipment, it will be in the battle strategy itself.

Paragraph 4: The smart military decision... advanced analysis under pressure
One of the biggest challenges in wars is making the right decision at the right time. In 2060, artificial intelligence provides fast and accurate analysis of the military situation. Weapons and drones rely not only on current information, but also on past data, such as enemy tactics and trends, allowing them to predict future movements. In critical moments, intelligent systems analyze all available options and offer the best strategy to achieve victory. Humans will be able to make quick decisions based on these analyses, reducing human errors and increasing the chances of success.

Paragraph 5: Self-propelled weapons and moral debate

But with this tremendous progress in artificial intelligence, an important question arises: Should drones and artificial intelligence be responsible for killing decisions? In 2060, despite their high accuracy and effectiveness, these weapons remain a matter of great controversy in military and political circles. Many experts warn of the danger of completely relying on intelligent systems to make combat decisions. Will we reach a day when humans become unnecessary in wars? The question opens a discussion about ethics and human values in future wars.

Military Robots: Revolution on the Battlefield

In the year 2060, military robots have become an essential part of the modern military, equipped with advanced artificial intelligence systems that enable them to operate in complex environments without the need for direct human intervention. These robots, which range from robotic infantry to armored vehicles and drones, have the ability to autonomously make field decisions based on intelligent analyzes performed by their systems. Thanks to artificial intelligence, military robots can identify targets with high accuracy, react to changing conditions on the battlefield, and coordinate with other units in the army to achieve the best possible outcome. This development enhances armies' ability to maneuver quickly, and significantly reduces human casualties, making military robots more effective in carrying out multiple tasks, whether attack, defense, or even reconnaissance.

Cyber Wars: The battle of intelligence against digital security

With the advancement of artificial intelligence, cyber warfare has evolved into a global threat in the 2060s. Although enemies can launch attacks online, artificial intelligence can now anticipate and respond to these attacks before they happen. Intelligent systems monitor data in real time and learn from any previous attack to devise new defensive methods. On the digital battlefield, where speed is king, AI can create complex offensive or defensive strategies in record time, making cybersecurity a priority in defending critical infrastructure. Smart tools can identify vulnerabilities before they are exploited, and analyze attackers' behavior to block or thwart their attempts in time.

Artificial intelligence and autonomous robots in military operations

Autonomous robots powered by artificial intelligence are becoming more capable of carrying out complex tasks in war zones. In 2060, these robots can operate separately from humans, but are still connected to command centers via sophisticated networks that ensure effective coordination. These robots can scout hostile areas, transport supplies, and even perform rescue operations on casualties on battlefields. Artificial intelligence provides these robots with the ability to make instant decisions based on incoming data, making them more efficient than ever before. For example, if part of the front lines is destroyed, robots can rearrange themselves to secure the position and perform alternative tasks on the fly, reducing the slowdown in military operations and increasing overall efficiency.

Air combat: drones and artificial intelligence

In 2060, drones are more advanced than ever, not only carrying out reconnaissance missions, but also performing sophisticated offensive and defensive actions. Drones powered by artificial intelligence are now able to identify, analyze, and interact with targets in real time, making them an extremely powerful tool in modern warfare. For example, drones can work in coordinated teams so that each drone can pinpoint the enemy's location, send alerts, and even deliver precision strikes. These operations rely on artificial intelligence to coordinate the movement of drones at a high level of efficiency, allowing the military to achieve success in air battles with minimal risk.

Artificial intelligence in managing multi-front wars

In 2060, artificial intelligence can manage wars on multiple fronts simultaneously, making warfare more integrated and effective. Intelligent systems monitor events in all domains—from land to sea to space—and make integrated decisions about how to allocate forces in real time. Information flows are analyzed and enemy threats are assessed across various platforms, providing military commanders with flexible and effective strategic options. This ability to coordinate between different fronts in an integrated manner ensures that future wars will be more coordinated and controlled than ever before, reducing the loss and strategic imbalance that occurred in traditional wars. At the same time, artificial intelligence allows generals to make critical decisions based on accurate information from all parties involved, allowing them to quickly change their plans if necessary.

—

Cyber defenses: a strong bulwark against cyber attacks

In the year 2060, cyber defenses have become one of the most powerful protective tools on the modern battlefield, using artificial intelligence to fend off cyber attacks with unprecedented intelligence and precision. Intelligent systems monitor data in real time and can analyze millions of points of information and identify potential attacks before they impact critical systems. Artificial Intelligence detects vulnerabilities in security systems and instantly develops new defensive methods to counter any new threats. These cyber defenses become more resilient and robust over time, as they learn from past attacks and adapt to be more efficient at preventing future attacks. This type of AI ensures that military and government networks are kept secure by countering the latest attack methods that enemies may use.

Digital espionage: exploiting artificial intelligence to collect information

With the development of artificial intelligence, digital espionage has become more precise and efficient in the 2060s. Intelligent systems are now used to infiltrate complex digital networks and analyze massive amounts of data to obtain sensitive information invisibly. Artificial intelligence can detect hidden patterns in encrypted messages, and search for vulnerabilities in security systems that may provide access to strategic information. With its ability to learn from every espionage attempt, AI becomes an almost undetectable tool that can exploit digital vulnerabilities quickly and effectively. Digital espionage is not limited to collecting information, but rather extends to analyzing data and utilizing it to enhance military capabilities, whether by understanding the enemy's movements or predicting its future strategies.

Intelligent surveillance systems: monitoring the enemy in real time

In 2060, AI-powered surveillance systems can monitor enemy movements in real time, continuously analyzing the information to detect any suspicious activity. Through the use of satellites, drones, and sensitive devices spread on the ground, artificial intelligence automatically tracks targets and analyzes data instantly. These systems can predict future enemy movements based on past behavioral patterns, helping military forces make informed strategic decisions. Furthermore, these systems are able to process huge amounts of data much faster than a human, making them better able to identify and respond to threats before they escalate.

Artificial Intelligence in Hacking Systems: Counterattack in Digital Warfare

In the world of digital warfare of 2060, artificial intelligence has become not only a defensive tool, but also an effective offensive tool. Intelligent systems can launch adverse attacks on enemy networks in real time, by penetrating digital systems and exploiting security vulnerabilities. These attacks are not limited to disrupting systems, but also include data manipulation or launching deceptive campaigns by hacking communication messages or electronic systems. Artificial intelligence can perform real-time analysis of an enemy attack and respond to it using innovative methods. Thanks to machine learning, adverse digital attacks can become more subtle and more impactful over time, making digital warfare more complex and violent.

Artificial intelligence in phishing attacks and digital disinformation

One innovative use of artificial intelligence in future warfare is the ability to carry out digital deception operations. AI can create complex webs of disinformation, intended to confuse and mislead the enemy about troop movements or attack strategies. Using artificial intelligence, enemy systems can be hacked and false or distorted information introduced, leading to wrong strategic decisions by the enemy military leadership. These deceptive operations may include simulating attacks or providing inaccurate reports that delay a response or change the enemy's military movements. Artificial intelligence makes these deception tactics more effective than ever before, as they can learn and improve through experience, creating a more uncertain and difficult war environment for the adversary.

—

Chapter Nine: Artificial Intelligence as a global force

Developed countries and their technological superiority

Artificial intelligence as an element in global conflicts

Cybersecurity and future wars

Chapter Nine: Artificial Intelligence as a global force

Developed countries and their technological superiority

In the world of 2060, artificial intelligence has become one of the main pillars on which developed countries build their technological and political power. With the increasing reliance on artificial intelligence in various fields such as medicine, industry, security, and trade, countries that invest heavily in this technology have begun to enhance their ability to lead the world. Developed countries with a strong AI infrastructure, such as the United States, China, and the European Union, have come to dominate the global political stage. These countries are not limited to using artificial intelligence to improve their daily lives, but are also working to use it as a strategic tool to expand their influence in various fields.

Artificial intelligence gives these countries an exceptional ability to analyze huge data and make quick decisions that affect the future of the world. In politics, these countries can use artificial intelligence to guide their geopolitical strategies, analyze trends in the global economy, and predict potential crises before they occur. In the military field, it can improve defense and control systems in an unprecedented way, enhancing its military power. Artificial intelligence also contributes to the sustainability of its economic growth by improving productivity in key sectors.

In addition, artificial intelligence in these countries has become a powerful tool to excel in the field of research and development. Research institutions in developed countries are working to develop intelligent systems that help discover solutions to complex problems, whether in the field of health, energy, or the environment. Perhaps the most obvious example of this is the significant progress in medical treatments using artificial intelligence, such as artificial intelligence used in drug design or in personalized medicine.

Data is one of the key factors that enable this technological power. Developed countries are investing heavily in building huge databases and advanced analysis centers to enable their smart systems to exploit this information in every aspect of their lives. These countries also have advanced security systems to protect their data and ensure its safe use in various fields, whether in the governmental, industrial, or commercial field.

With the advancement of artificial intelligence, developed countries have begun to promote public-private partnerships, where smart systems in different industries are strategically integrated. Major companies in these countries are developing innovative products that rely heavily on artificial intelligence, making them more competitive on a global level. Through these partnerships, production methods are improved, and innovative solutions to economic challenges are provided, which increases the ability of these countries to maintain their leadership in the global economy.

However, with this enormous technological capacity, there are also the ethical and political challenges that developed countries may face in the context of artificial intelligence. The more advanced this technology is, the greater the need to ensure that it is used fairly and ethically. For example, the issue of privacy rights, the use of artificial intelligence in security, and data governance may raise a lot of controversy in these countries. It will be essential in the coming years for developed countries to find ways to codify the use of AI in line with their humanitarian values.

Ultimately, it can be said that AI in 2060 will become not only an engine of economic growth and technological progress, but also a major instrument of geopolitical power. The countries that will invest intensively in this field are the ones that will still be able to maintain their position on the global stage, both politically and economically. This technological superiority will be the foundation upon which future strategies are built to determine the course of the world in the coming decades.

Artificial Intelligence as a Critical Element in Global Conflicts: The New Balance of Power

In the year 2060, artificial intelligence has become more than just a technology, but rather the cornerstone of changing the global balance of power. Artificial intelligence has introduced a new element in international warfare, where technology is intertwined with military strategies, creating a radical shift in the way countries deal with each other. The struggle between major powers no longer takes place only on traditional battlefields, but also on digital fronts. Artificial intelligence weapons, such as drones equipped with advanced algorithms that can autonomously identify military targets, and cyberattacks carried out by intelligent systems that control the flow of information, have become crucial tools on the global battlefield.

With the development of these technologies, artificial intelligence has become a more reliable strategic weapon than ever before. Countries that control this technology are able to use artificial intelligence not only in war, but also in managing complex economic conflicts and international relations. These major powers are guiding global shifts in trade, energy, and politics by using artificial intelligence to analyze data and predict future trends, giving them an unprecedented ability to impose their will on the world.

Artificial Intelligence in Cyberwarfare: A New Unseen Battlefield

At the heart of modern global conflicts, artificial intelligence appears as an invisible force, driven by algorithms and big data, leaving traces in the digital world that no one can see except through its devastating consequences. Cyber wars waged over the Internet are becoming more complex and bloody. AI systems infiltrate enemy networks invisibly, hijack data and game the entire system without anyone noticing. In these digital wars, billions of data points are analyzed in moments, and artificial intelligence identifies weaknesses in the enemy's digital defenses. Through sophisticated ransomware attacks, or disruption of power grids, AI bots can leave entire countries in disarray.

These digital attacks are no longer just targeting technical infrastructure, but have become a tool for changing the international balance of power. Countries that possess offensive defensive capabilities based on artificial intelligence can put competing countries under unprecedented pressure, not through traditional military force, but through hidden strikes that destroy vital systems in moments. With this digital transformation, every device and every data point becomes a battlefield that can be hacked or exploited.

Artificial Intelligence in Smart Weapons: Non-Human Combat

In the world of future warfare, artificial intelligence is beginning to become a major driver of smart weapons. Drones, combat robots, and autonomous weapons that make autonomous decisions are becoming an integral part of future militaries. In 2060, the human soldier will no longer need to intervene constantly. Everything, from identifying targets to executing precise strikes, is done using algorithms trained to handle complex situations in live combat. What makes this mode even more exciting is that these smart weapons learn and adapt quickly, making it very difficult for enemies to predict their movements.

These weapons are not only limited to destroying the enemy, but have become an invisible threat in the conflict. When war becomes governed by artificial intelligence, the rules of the game change radically. Can conventional armies keep up with these unmanned weapons? Or will artificial intelligence be the actual ruler of the military future?

Economic Wars: How Artificial Intelligence is Changing the Balance of Economic Power

The effects of artificial intelligence are not limited to the military battlefield only, but rather its impact extends to the arenas of global economic conflicts. In the future, artificial intelligence will become an unprecedented tool for analyzing financial markets, and will become the main factor in making strategic economic decisions. The major countries that control artificial intelligence will be able to impose their dominance on global markets, by moving financial markets in a precise manner, and directing investment flows in unexpected ways. Artificial intelligence can spot new business opportunities before they arise, giving these countries a huge competitive advantage in the global economy.

But what happens when the economy itself becomes a battlefield? Developed countries will strive to dominate AI technology, which will lead to an invisible economic arms race. Intelligent algorithms will be used to direct economic wars, and economic policies will become a precise and impenetrable tool for pressure on rival nations.

Artificial Intelligence in Media Wars: Shaping Public Opinion in Moments

One of the most profound aspects of the impact of artificial intelligence in global conflicts is its use in information wars. In the future, artificial intelligence will be used not only to analyze data, but also to direct complex advertising campaigns aimed at shaping public opinion. Intelligent systems can create personalized advertising content that targets individuals at the moment their minds are most affected. States will be able to sow chaos and disinformation among enemy ranks by targeting certain categories of people with disinformation or propaganda, completely diverting the course of the conflict. As artificial intelligence develops, media wars become more exciting and interesting, as each side strives to keep its opponent in a state of confusion and doubt.

Cybersecurity and Future Wars 2060," focusing on the excitement and expected implications:

---

1. A battlefield without armies: The world is burning behind screens

In the year 2060, wars are no longer fought only on Earth, but screens have become the new battlefields. We no longer see soldiers advancing towards the enemy, but digital codes hurtling like missiles to destroy the vital systems of entire countries. Cyber attacks have become an effective tool to cripple banks, airports, hospitals and even power plants. Here, no shots are heard, but rather sirens demanding that the system be stopped immediately! Behind keyboards, fierce battles are being waged that shape the fate of countries.

---

2. Artificial Intelligence...the hidden soldier in the network war

Imagine that there is an "electronic soldier" who never sleeps or gets tired, who learns from every attack and improves every second. This is artificial intelligence in cybersecurity. In 2060, humans are no longer the only ones defending systems, but are joined by intelligent programs capable of detecting threats before they occur. These systems can respond to a cyberattack in milliseconds, identify its source, and direct a counterattack. A game of cat and mouse between two artificial intelligences, one attacking and the other defending!

---

3. When information becomes a weapon

In the wars of the future, information equals power. Artificial intelligence systems analyze billions of data and detect the intentions of other countries before they speak them. A country leaking fake information to mislead the enemy? In 2060, artificial intelligence can detect disinformation in moments. But what is even more dangerous is using the same technology to falsify facts, guide people, and sow chaos! Information warfare has become more deadly than bombs, because it attacks the mind first.

---

4. Countries collapse...with just one button!

Can you imagine that an entire country could be plunged into darkness with just the push of a button? In 2060, this is no longer a fantasy. Cyber attacks can disrupt the power grid, control traffic systems, shut down water plants, and even silence communications networks. Here, cybersecurity has become every country's first defense. The real race is no longer just over who has the strongest army, but rather over who has the strongest electronic protection system.

---

5. Is there a safe front in 2060?

In this fast-paced era, no one is safe. Individuals, companies, and even governments are all potential targets in these cyberwars. Terrorist organizations, hidden armies, and even individuals obsessed with sabotage all have dangerous tools thanks to artificial intelligence. Therefore, the future of cybersecurity depends on the extent of our preparedness, cooperation, and continuous development of these intelligent systems. The next hero may not be an army commander, but a young programmer who saved his country from digital collapse.

—

11. Chapter Ten: Future challenges and risks

Job loss and social impact

Ethical and legal concerns

The need for unified international legislation

"Job Loss and Social Impact 2060" from Chapter 10: Future Challenges and Risks:

---

1. The dream of artificial intelligence... and the nightmare of humans

Initially, the world welcomed the AI revolution as a sign of progress and convenience. Machines are becoming more accurate, faster to produce, and less expensive than humans. But this dream did not come without a price. In 2060, millions of traditional jobs have quietly disappeared. Bank employees, drivers, and even teachers are being replaced by smart systems that work around the clock. You don't need a salary, you don't need a vacation, and you don't need to be late for work. But this progress swept away the dreams of many people, leaving a social vacuum that widened day after day. The question that worries everyone has become: "Does the future belong only to machines?"

2. The collapse of the middle class...the beginning of the disintegration of societies?

In 2060, the problem is no longer just unemployment, but the disappearance of the "middle class" that represented stability. This class, which includes employees, craftsmen, and service workers, is disappearing. For every job that goes to a machine, a real person loses their livelihood, and society loses its balance. With this collapse, a sharp division began to appear: a few own the technology and control the economy, and a majority suffers from a loss of financial security. Markets began to shrink, demand declined, and the global economy began to feel the cold coming from the heart of the technological revolution.

3. Psychological impact: An entire generation without a goal

The problem is not only the loss of income, but the loss of meaning. In the 2060s, signs of a mass psychological crisis began to emerge, especially among young people. After years of study and fatigue, the young man finds himself facing a wall: no jobs, no opportunity, only an artificial intelligence that has mastered everything he has learned. This feeling of helplessness and uselessness creates a dangerous psychological vacuum, pushing some to isolate, and others to rebel or even deviate. Societies that do not prepare their children for this new reality may face breakdowns in relationships and a loss of confidence in the future.

4. Are we rehabilitating people...or marginalizing them?

In the face of this radical change, countries began to react differently. Some governments have initiated training programs to rehabilitate workers and teach them new skills in line with the age of artificial intelligence. But the challenge was huge: not everyone can learn programming or data analysis. What about the elderly? What about those with manual skills? On the other hand, other countries ignored the crisis, which led to the emergence of completely marginalized groups. And the result? A feeling of discrimination and social tension that may turn into real unrest.

5. Do we rule the machines or do they rule us?

The most dangerous question in 2060 is no longer just about jobs, but about power. Who controls artificial intelligence? Who decides who will work and who will be replaced? If the decision falls into the hands of large technology companies, are we entering a new era of digital colonialism? If fair laws and systems that balance technology and social justice are not put in place, we may find ourselves in a world governed not by law, but by codes. And perhaps, at some point, we'll realize that we've created something we can't stop... and that the real threat wasn't the machine itself, but our oversight of it.

Ethical and legal concerns

Subject:
"Ethical and Legal Concerns – 2060" within Chapter Ten: Future Challenges and Risks:

---

1. Who holds the artificial mind accountable?

In 2060, artificial intelligence has become more than just a tool. It has become a decision maker in sensitive areas: from diagnosing diseases, to determining who gets a loan, or who accepts a job. But here a serious question arises: What if he made a mistake? Who is legally responsible? In a world governed by algorithms, responsibility is no longer clear. Do we blame the programmer? Company? Or the system itself? This legal gap threatens the idea of justice, and opens the door to a chaos of unjust decisions, without anyone being held accountable.

---

2. Justice in the age of algorithms

The scary thing about AI is that it "seems" objective, but in reality it reflects human-made biases. In the 2060s, many scandals emerged of algorithms that discriminate against certain groups, whether in terms of race, gender, or even social background. If the future is determined by an intelligence we do not fully understand, can we trust its outcomes? If these algorithms become part of the justice, policing, or employment system, we may find ourselves living in an unjust technological world.

---

3. Does the machine have a conscience?

In the world of 2060, machines interact with us, smile, and have full conversations. But it lacks something essential: conscience. The machine does not feel guilt, nor does it understand human pain. As we become more dependent on them, we risk losing the human side of our decisions. What if a self-driving car decided to run over

one person to save five? Is this an ethical decision? Or cold calculation? These
.dilemmas show that AI may be powerful... but heartless

?Privacy...a currency of the past .4

With every step we take in 2060, there is a camera watching, an app recording, or an
algorithm analyzing. Artificial intelligence feeds on data, and the more it knows about
us, the more accurate it becomes. But this means that our private lives are completely
exposed. Does any system have the right to know everything about you? From your
friends, to your preferences, to your health record? Privacy has transformed from a
human right into a rare luxury. The real danger is that people may become
.accustomed to this surveillance... and accept it without resistance

---

Between freedom and control .5

Artificial intelligence in 2060 is a powerful tool, but it may become a dangerous
weapon in the hands of whoever possesses it. Some countries began using it to
monitor their people, control their opinions, and direct their political and economic
choices without them realizing it. Here concerns arise: Is artificial intelligence used as
a means to liberate humans... or as a means to control them? The battle is no longer
just over technology, but over our values as a human race: freedom, dignity, and
justice. The stakes are big... Either we adapt artificial intelligence to serve us, or we
.become its servants

—

?Conclusion: Are we prepared for the future

By the end of this book, we will have taken a long and exciting journey into the world
of 2060, where artificial intelligence has become part of everything around us. We
started with commerce, and we saw how smart stores became, and how machines
make accurate decisions in buying and selling, then we entered the world of industry,
agriculture, tourism, transportation, and even the military fields. Each season was like
a window into a new form of life, a life that moves quickly, thinks intelligently, and
.constantly changes

But in all of these chapters, the real question was not only: "Where has AI been?" but
"?rather, the most important question was: "Where are we going
Will people live more comfortably thanks to this technology? Or will he find himself in
?a difficult race to maintain his place amid this massive boom
Will human values such as justice, freedom, and cooperation remain strong in this
?future? Or will you dissolve into a world controlled by algorithms and cold decisions

We have seen the great positive effects of this development: speed, accuracy, convenience, production, development... But we have also seen another, no less important side: fear of job loss, class division, ethical problems, loss of privacy, and the increasing control of technology over the details of our lives.

Artificial intelligence in 2060 is like a double-edged sword: it may be the greatest achievement known to man, and it may be the beginning of a major challenge facing the entire world.

In the end, the decision remains in our hands: Will we use this power to serve people and humanity? Or will we let it control us without awareness or preparation?

This book does not close with an end point, but rather opens with a big question for every reader:

How will we be part of this future? What role will we play in a world moving at the speed of light?

The future is not far away...it is closer than we imagine. Let us prepare for it with a conscious heart, an alert mind, and an unwavering conscience.